SPIRIT-LIFTING THOUGHTS FOR EVERY DAY OF THE YEAR

Daily Guideposts 2005

Rejoicing in Hope . . .

DAILY GUIDEPOSTS, 2005 is an astonishing, faith-building book of 365 brand-new daily devotionals. It is filled from cover to cover with inspiring true stories of everyday life, uplifting Bible verses and personal prayers.

Our theme for *DAILY GUIDEPOSTS, 2005* is "Rejoicing in Hope." Throughout the year, you'll discover 7 special series by people from all walks of life who are ready to share their own joys and sorrows with the *Daily Guideposts* family, and to show you the ways the Lord has helped them to rejoice in hope.

DAILY GUIDEPOSTS, 2005 is available in both regular print and large print editions. Imagine . . . 365 daily doses of inspiration only from Guideposts.

✱ *Turn to the "Fellowship Corner," at the back of the book, where you'll meet the sixty contributors.*

✱ *Scan the Scripture Reference Index and Authors, Titles and Subjects Index to help you locate your favorite verses and topics.*

✱ *Meet a different reader each month in "Reader's Room," where people like you share their experiences of God's blessings in their lives.*

✱ *Enjoy monthly journal pages and original artwork.*

Return the Free Examination Certificate for a FREE 30-day preview of *DAILY GUIDEPOSTS, 2005* . . . and receive a FREE *Scripture Bookmark.*

Free SCRIPTURE BOOKMARK *—just for ordering!*

Rejoice in the Lord alway: and again I say, Rejoice.

Complete the
Free Examination Certificate
and mail today for
your 30-Day Preview.

FREE EXAMINATION CERTIFICATE

YES! Please rush me *DAILY GUIDEPOSTS, 2005* at no risk or obligation, to examine FREE for 30 days. If I decide to keep it, I will be billed at the low Guideposts price of $14.95, plus shipping and processing. If not completely satisfied, I may return the book within 30 days and owe nothing. *As a FREE BONUS with each book, I will receive a Scripture Bookmark.*

Total copies ordered: _____

Regular Print ___ copies (hardcover)   Large Print ___ copies (softcover)

Please print your name and address:

_____
NAME

_____
ADDRESS   APT#

_____
CITY   STATE   ZIP

Allow 4 weeks for delivery. Orders subject to credit approval.
Send no money now. We will bill you later.
www.guidepostsbooks.com

Printed in USA
16/202245306

No need to send money now!

ideals®
THANKSGIVING

SEPTEMBER 2004

Dedicated to a celebration—through poetry and prose—of the American ideals of faith in God, loyalty to country, and love of family.

A single thankful thought toward heaven is the most perfect of all prayers.
—Gotthold Ephraim Lessing

IDEALS—Vol 61, No. 5 September 2004 IDEALS (ISSN 0019-137X, USPS 256-240) is published six times a year: January, March, May, July, September, and November by IDEALS PUBLICATIONS, a division of Guideposts, 39 Seminary Hill Road, Carmel, NY 10512. Copyright © 2004 by IDEALS PUBLICATIONS, a division of Guideposts. All rights reserved. The cover and entire contents of IDEALS are fully protected by copyright and must not be reproduced in any manner whatsoever. Title IDEALS registered U.S. Patent Office. Printed and bound in USA. Printed on Weyerhaeuser Husky. The paper used in this publication meets the minimum requirements of American National Standard for Information Sciences—Permanence of Paper for Printed Library Materials, ANSI Z39.48-1984. Periodicals postage paid at Carmel, New York, and additional mailing offices. Canadian mailed under Publications Mail Agreement Number 40010140. POSTMASTER: Send address changes to Ideals, 39 Seminary Hill Road, Carmel, NY 10512. CANADA POST: Send address changes to Guideposts PO Box 1051, Fort Erie ON L2A 6C7. For subscription or customer service questions, contact Ideals Publications, a division of Guideposts, 39 Seminary Hill Road, Carmel, NY 10512. Fax 845-228-2115. Reader Preference Service: We occasionally make our mailing lists available to other companies whose products or services might interest you. If you prefer not to be included, please write to Ideals Customer Service.

ISBN 0-8249-1234-9   GST 893989236

Visit the *Ideals* website at www.idealsbooks.com

Cover: This spectacular maple is the centerpiece of the town square in Bishop Hill, Henry County, Illinois. Photograph by Mary Liz Austin/Donnelly Austin Photography.

Inside front cover: This lovely autumn painting is entitled NATURE MORTE AUX RAISINS, by Alexis Kreyder (1839-1912). Image provided by Fine Art Photographic Library, Ltd., London/Waterhouse & Dodd.

Inside back cover: The beautiful bounty of the season overflows this yard on a bright autumn afternoon in AUTUMN JOY by Diane Phalen. Painting © Diane Phalen Watercolors.

In This Issue

Golden Days
G. C. Compton

If I could but relive
Just one golden day again,
I would not waste the sunrise
Nor shut away the wind—
But open wide my window,
Spring the latch upon my door,
To each leaf and tiny raindrop,
To every footstep on my floor.
Would that I had learned,
Ere precious moments slipped away,
To wait not on tomorrow—
For today's my golden day.

Autumn
Wilmer E. Bresee

It's autumn on the hilltops
With gold enough for all;
A fortune in the treetops,
So bright on leaves that fall.
Each tree outdoes its fellow
In the colors of its gown,
With crimson, gold, and yellow,
And deep and priceless brown.
Distant knolls are frosty white;
There's a keen edge to the breeze
That hums low through the still night
And tiptoes through the trees.

A breathtaking view of Camden, Maine, from Mount Battle.
Photograph by Dick Dietrich/Dietrich Leis Stock Photography.

I trust in Nature for the stable laws

Of beauty and utility. Spring shall plant

And Autumn garner to the end of time.

I trust in God—the right shall be the right

And other than the wrong while He endures.

I trust in my own soul, that can perceive

The outward and the inward—Nature's good

And God's. —ROBERT BROWNING

Autumn in the West

William Davis Gallagher

Deep murmurs from the trees, bending with brown
And ripened mast, are interrupted oft
By sounds of dropping nuts; and warily
The turkey from the thicket comes, and swift
As flies an arrow darts the pheasant down,
To batten on the autumn; and the air,
At times, is darkened by a sudden rush
Of myriad wings, as the wild pigeon leads
His squadrons to the banquet. Far away,
Where tranquil groves on sunny slopes supply
Their liberal store of fruits, the merry laugh
Of children and the truant schoolboy's shout
Ring on the air, as, from the hollows borne,
Nuts load their creaking carts, and lush pawpaws
Their motley baskets fill, with clustering grapes
And golden-sphered persimmons spread o'er all.

The majesty of the land is evident in these snow-covered peaks in Uncompahgre National Forest in Colorado. Photograph by Christopher Talbot Frank.

Panorama

Carolyn Melbye

Brilliant rust and scarlet cloaks
Are weighing down the arms of oaks,
While up and down the dusty road
Lie mounds of aspens' lovely gold.
The birches white and stately stand,
Lending their glow on every hand.
Orange and flame are the maples' crowns,
Fragile and light, fluttering down.
But the pines remain unchanged, serene,
Forming the background of evergreen.

Days of Splendor

Elisabeth Weaver Winstead

The first bronze leaf dropped down today;
Yellow butterflies are still at play.
The sun makes footprints on the ground;
Lush fruit trees flaunt rich jeweled crowns.

Through gilded fire thorn's tawny shade,
Maples wave leaf banners on parade.
Bright orange persimmons on woodland trees
Invite thick clouds of honeybees.

On country trails, white birches shine;
Deep emerald tones are etched on pines;
Spry squirrels hide treasured acorns found
From towering oak to leaf-strewn ground.

Proud harvest proved a bountiful yield,
A rich cornucopia from valley and field;
Our hearts are filled with joyful praise
For the radiant splendor of rare autumn days.

This three-story reproduction of a log barn and buggy shed is at Luxenhaus Farm, Marthasville, Missouri. Photograph by Jessie Walker.

Overleaf: Aspen trees near Hart Prairie Road, Flagstaff, Arizona, in their fall finery, offer a reflective moment for those who take the time to observe. Photograph by Dick Dietrich/Dietrich Leis Stock Photography.

Painting the Hills
Wilmer E. Bresee

I walked along a road today,
Outside the city's bounds,
Where hills that yesterday were green
And echoed shrill bird sounds
Have donned a new and bright array
Not made in any human mills,
And thought, "Soon, now,
      the birds will go,
When Autumn paints the hills."

There were the stately maple trees
Decked out in gaudy hues,
The pond that slept nearby
Gave back the heavens' blues.
I saw a nearby farmhouse too,
With flowers by its sills;
But their colors couldn't equal those
That Autumn gave the hills.

Far above, in the distance clear,
Was a white October cloud,
Scurrying on before the wind
To which the cornstalks bowed,
Before the wind that swept my thoughts
Quite free of earthly ills.
For beauty leaves no room for gloom
When Autumn paints the hills.

Autumn's Art
Joyce Inman Moore

When Autumn came strolling the hill and the dell,
She fashioned the landscape and fashioned it well,
With pigment of scarlet and rich-minted gold,
Imparting a mural for all to behold.

She clad the chrysanthemums in a deft way;
And, proud as a princess in courtly array,
She wakened late rosebuds with spangles of dew
And rouged each cheek well before she was through.

From sapphire decanter she poured on the sky
A colorful spectacle, kind to the eye.
Then for a quaint encore she piped a sweet tune
While placing a halo above the bright moon.

As I stood watching, there fell on the air
A reverent hush, as sedate as a prayer,
And star tapers glowed on the chapel of night,
When Autumn came ushering such a grand sight.

In Great Smoky Mountains National Park, near Bryson City, North Carolina, the palette of early fall colors has touched the upper elevations. Photograph by Mary Liz Austin/Donnelly Austin Photography.

CHANGING SEASONS

Shirley Sallay

I think the forest is waiting today
    for a changing of the wind;
She knows that she is seeing now
    a beautiful summer's end.

The birds are bidding fond farewell
    and soaring on their way;
They've been preparing many weeks
    for this departure day.

Flowers are resplendent
    with last sweet blossoms now,
While shrubs and trees in crimson, gold,
    are taking their deep, final bow.

Creatures scurry underfoot,
    gathering acorns and berries and such,
Chattering loudly all the time
    and lending a comic touch

To the sadness that we all do sense
    when summer fades away
And fall takes up her palette
    to begin her grand display.

AUTUMN MAGIC

Virginia Borman Grimmer

Once again it's autumn,
And there's nothing quite so grand
As a swath of vibrant color
Is brushed across the land.
There's magic in the season,
The regal one of fall,
When the purple grapes hang heavy
On the arbor's weathered wall.
Painted leaves of scarlet
Make umbrellas of the trees
That shimmer in the sunshine
As the gentle breezes tease.
Baskets heaped with apples
And pumpkins, orange and round,
Rest beside the country lanes
Where Queen Anne's lace abounds.
In the corner of the garden,
Curly parsley grows yet green,
Right beside the chrysanthemums
That so enhance the scene.
Yes, once again it's autumn
And great beauty does unfold,
As the Master of the seasons
Gives us richer gifts than gold.

GOD'S LABEL

Charlotte Partin

Horizons, hand-hemmed
With rickrack of trees,
Gold sunbeams threaded
Through pleats of the seas,
Puff-quilted clouds
Cross-stitched in lamés—
These are the marks
God stamps on His days.

This lovely valley of East Orange, Vermont, is surrounded by a bright autumn panorama. Photograph by F. Sieb/H. Armstrong Roberts.

When Acorns Fall
Alfred Austin

When acorns fall, and swallows troop for flight,
And hope, matured slowly, mellows to regret,
And Autumn, pressed by Winter for his debt,
Drops leaf on leaf till she be beggared quite;
Should then the crescent moon's unselfish light
Gleam up the sky just as the sun doth set,
Her brightening gaze, though day and dark have met,
Prolongs the gloaming and retards the night.
So, fair young life, new-risen upon mine,
Just as it owns the edict of decay
And Fancy's fires should pale and pass away,
My menaced glory takes a glow from thine,
And, in the deepening sundown of my day,
Thou with thy dawn delayest my decline.

Treasures
Vincent Godfrey Burns

What magic there is in the wand
Which autumn wields
When it pours its stream of gold
On the harvest fields:
A loveliness tinting all
That shines to the eyes,
With purple curtains of haze
Let down from the skies;
The maples with flaming banners
In every wood,
The cornstalks like ranks
Of a rustic brotherhood;

The barns all bursting with grain
As the apples fall,
And a wondrous peace
Seems somehow part of it all.
There are rainbow colors
Mirrored in placid streams,
And earth is hushed
To a music of whispers and dreams.
The bees are filling their hives
With a dusty gold,
And the heart is filled
With more than a heart can hold.

*A big-leaf maple drapes over the South Fork of the McKenzie River in
Willamette National Forest, Lane County, Oregon. Photograph by Steve Terrill.*

BITS & PIECES

*Traveler, take heed for journeys undertaken in the dark of the year.
Go in the bright blaze of autumn's equinox.*

—*Margaret Abigail Walker*

*That night was the turning point in the season. We
had gone to bed in summer, and we awoke in autumn;
for summer passes into autumn in some imaginable
point of time, like the turning of a leaf.*

—*Henry David Thoreau*

*There is a harmony
In autumn, and a lustre in its sky,
Which through the summer is not heard or seen,
As if it could not be, as if it had not been!*

—*Percy Bysshe Shelley*

*Boughs are daily rifled
By the gusty thieves,
And the book of nature
Getteth short of leaves.*

—*Thomas Hood*

*I*n the autumn brilliance
feathers tingle at fingertips.
—*Denise Levertov*

*A*utumn resumes the land, ruffles the
woods with smoky wings, entangles them.
—*Geoffrey Hill*

*W*hat is autumn?
A second spring, where the leaves imitate the flowers.
—*Albert Camus*

*A*utumn's the mellow time.
—*William Allingham*

*T*he apples are all getting tinted
In the cool light of autumn.
—*John Ashbery*

*T*he American spring is by no means so agreeable as
the American autumn; both move with faltering step,
and slow; but this lingering pace, which is delicious in
autumn, is most tormenting in the spring.
—*Frances Trollope*

I saw old autumn in the misty morn
Stand shadowless like silence, listening to silence.
—*Thomas Hood*

Gypsy
Kay Hoffman

I lose my heart to Autumn—
It happens every year;
For Autumn is but a gypsy,
So full of warmth and cheer.

Dressed in dazzling red and gold,
Strolling over hill and way,
She flaunts her beauty unabashed
And draws all eyes her way.

The queen of every harvest ball,
By Mother Nature crowned,
A spendthrift at the county fair,
She flings her jewels around.

I know that Autumn's clever—
For her I'm easy prey;
She beckons with a warm, bright smile
And steals my heart away.

Love in Autumn
Oliver Jenkins

My love will come in autumn-time
When leaves go spinning to the ground
And wistful stars in heaven chime
With the leaves' soft sound.

Then we shall walk through dusty lanes
And pause beneath low-hanging boughs,
And there, while soft-hued beauty reigns,
We'll make our vows.

Let others seek in spring for sighs
When love flames forth from every seed;
But love that blooms when nature dies
Is love indeed!

*In Skagit River Valley, Washington, a small chapel is
surrounded by the gold of big-leaf maples. Photograph
by Terry Donnelly/Donnelly Austin Photography.*

The Gold of Fall

Ruth Roberts Douglas

Golden leaves are floating down.
They crunch beneath my feet,
Drift in banks against the fence,
And dance along the street.
Neighbors rake them into heaps
And stack them just like hay,
But teasing breezes lift them up
And carry them away.
Golden sunlight filters through
The treetops overhead,
Picks up gold in Tabby's coat
And in my flower bed.
The golden band on Mother's hand
Gleams like a star at night,
While gold threads in her auburn hair
Shine brighter than the light.
The harvest moon, a yellow cheese,
Beams down like copper mint
On rows of pumpkins stacked beside
The farmer's split-rail fence.
My gold retriever seems to sense
That fall is in the air
And chases dust that goldenrods
Are sprinkling everywhere.

Pumpkins filling a boat on a roadside near Chester, Vermont, give passersby a pleasant surprise. Photograph by William H. Johnson.

TRAVELER'S DIARY

Marie H. Andrews

PRINCETON UNIVERSITY CHAPEL
PRINCETON, NEW JERSEY

There are many beautiful houses of worship within the United States, but my favorite, outside of my home church, is one our family found by one of those accidental decisions made on a vacation. From New York City, my teenage daughter and I chose to be adventurous and ride the train from Penn Station to Princeton Junction in order to visit Princeton University.

Tours of the campus are led by undergraduates called Orange Key guides and are offered every day of the week except during winter holidays or on major holidays.

Even though I thought the Putnam Memorial sculptures at various locations throughout the campus were fascinating, particularly "Head of a Woman" by Pablo Picasso, I was still able to absorb some of the interesting history that our guide summarized for us as we walked toward the massive University Chapel.

Princeton University is one of the oldest universities in the United States, founded in 1746 by the Presbyterian Synod and first known as the College of New Jersey. After the unfortunate destruction of the university's chapel by fire in 1920, Ralph Adams Cram was hired as the supervising architect of the new chapel. As an outstanding architect focusing on the Gothic style, he designed the building to be a "storybook of the Christian faith," our guide informed us.

As we approached the chapel, the limestone pinnacles and the Gothic arches created an instant feeling of magnitude and reverence. The exterior is made of Pennsylvania sandstone with Indiana limestone trim, as well as granite, giving the chapel the look of massive stability. The guide told us that the construction took three years at a cost of more than two million dollars to complete. Today there are special services of music, thanksgiving, and penitence, as well as marriages, baptisms, and funerals which take place here. Interestingly enough, our guide also told us that several of the

I was moved by the magnificent union of art and literature in the expression of worship.

men working for Cram were Yale graduates and that they carved a scowling bulldog on one drainpipe. Other whimsical figures, carved by Irish and Italian laborers, decorate other downspouts.

When we entered the chapel, everyone in our tour group quieted as each individual noted the Nativity window in the narthex, the front hall of the building. Christ is depicted as being watched over by Mary and Joseph. Our guide explained that this window demonstrates the importance of family. Charles J. Connick, a famous designer of stained glass, was commissioned to create the windows for the chapel.

As we continued toward the nave, the largest part of the chapel, we walked by the beautiful rows of pews that our guide told us were carved from Civil War gun carriages.

We stopped in front of the pulpit, where each wing of the building's two axes are visible. The four massive stained-glass windows at each end are all visible at this place. Endurance, the theme of the north window, depicts Christ surrounded by the martyrs of the church; the east window's theme of Love shows Christ at the Last Supper; the south window portrays Christ as the Teacher, with teachers and philosophers surrounding him. One of these, our guide pointed out, is John Witherspooon, the sixth president of the university and the only clergyman to sign the Declaration of Independence. The fourth window, rising over the entrance, depicts Christ in Heaven. The guide informed us that there are more than ten thousand square feet of leaded glass in the entire chapel. Light filtering through the glass hundreds of feet above us seemed to dwarf us all and yet offered a feeling of awe tempered with peace.

In the Milbank chancel, named after a benefactor, in addition to the enormous organ, the beautifully carved choir pews sedately await the renowned Chapel Choir. Originally an all-male chorus, the Chapel Choir now includes women and is made up of undergraduate and graduate students and faculty, who must audition for positions. As a former English teacher, I was awed by the six smaller windows in this chancel. The first two represent psalms of David and the others, cycles from four great Christian literary works: Paul Bunyan's *Pilgrim's Progress*, Dante's *Comedia*, Malory's *Le Morte d'Arthur*, and John Milton's *Paradise Lost*. I was moved by the magnificent union of art and literature in the expression of worship.

My daughter noticed a carving of a seeing-eye dog, among all the elaborate detailed woodwork-

Light filters through the magnificent stained-glass windows in Princeton University Chapel. Stained-glass designs by Charles J. Connick. Photograph by R. Krubner/H. Armstrong Roberts.

ing, and asked the guide about its origins. It seems that the carving honors a Princeton alumnus who founded the worldwide service, and it is a favorite of children who visit the chapel.

My daughter also was intrigued by a modern element, the large liturgical banners and paintings on silk done by artist Juanita Yoder Kauffmann. The artist used abstract forms and patterns of swirling color that blend beautifully with the chapel's light.

On the train ride back to New York City, my daughter and I quietly discussed the many ways that man has found to acknowledge the presence of God in his life. From the simple wooden structures of the early colonies to this example of the superb achievement of many talented and inspired people coming together, each has its own particular way of helping us worship.

Swish, Crackle, Crunch

Rose Gleisberg

Hey!
Aren't you
the same leaf
that dangled from my
maple tree last week, the one
that swung from bough to bough,
then unraveled from intertwined twigs
and tumbled to layers of other leaf beds?
Aren't you the leaf my children
slipped on while playing hide-and-seek,
the one they strolled and rolled on when raking
you into a pile? Why, it is you! I remember
your splashes of amber and red, like a jeweled crown
sparkling through the morning frost. We
felt the wind swish you right onto my son's brown
mitten, lying still and uncurled.
All the other leaves in their collage of colors
crackled in our fingers and crunched when we
plunged into raked piles, but you
sailed on your own sea of bark and branches
landing as softly as a blanket on a baby.
Once you bowed to the passersby from your bough,
and now you bow to me on my doorstep,
twirling from your stem,
flowing into my hand
like
a

s

t

r

e

a

m.

Maple Leaves

Beverly McLoughland

The leafy ceiling
Of the maple tree
Spreads wide and golden
Over me.
It looks as though
The branches hold
A hundred million
Leaves of gold.
A hundred million
Leaves or more—
Less one . . .
Or two . . .
Or three . . .
Or four. . . .

*Above right: A silver maple leaf is caught on blades of Japanese
silver grass on Sauvie Island in Columbia County, Oregon. Photograph by Steve Terrill.*

*A vine maple displays its fall wardrobe in Mount Baker-Snoqualmie National Forest,
Washington. Photograph by Terry Donnelly/Donnelly Austin Photography.*

Dancing Leaves

Louise Valley

The wind is whistling
　　Through the trees;
It plays a tune
　　For dancing leaves.
They swing and sway
　　Around, around,
Dancing till they
　　Touch the ground.
A little leaf here,
　　A little leaf there,
Until the branches
　　All are bare.
Then winter's frost
　　Completes the show,
And dancing leaves
　　Are covered with snow.

An Autumn Breeze

William Hamilton Hayne

This gentle and half-melancholy breeze
Is but a wandering Hamlet of the trees,
Who finds a tongue in every lingering leaf
To voice some subtlety of sylvan grief.

Begin with Wind

Evelyn Tooley Hunt

Begin with wind:
Wind breathing on the land,
Whispering life into the mangrove trees,
Gentling the cypress buds to ecstasies
Of green, lifting the yucca stalk to stand
Tall in the salty sand.
Begin with rain:
Parting the marshes where the sea has spun
Long threads of silver, and where seeds have lain,
Washing the channels where their roots will run.
Begin with sun:
Day springing out of night,
Waking the dormant gold of jasmine,
Shaping the orange and the tangerine
To its own image and to man's delight.
Praise wind and rain and sun, and seed and pod;
But when the praise begins, begin with God.

The Ausable River in Adirondack Park and Preserve, New York, is bordered by jewel-toned trees. Photograph by Christopher Talbot Frank.

READERS' REFLECTIONS

First Snowing
Stan Thawley
St. Louis, Missouri

Slowly the first few flakes now float down,
Like faint fluttering wings of small white doves.
They come dream-drifting, smooth as soft slippers,
Like pure, silent notes on thin, airy edges.
Like gowns dancing down, feather veils falling,
Quiet white sifting of small pirouettes.
Some swirl and twirl in fast rising rushes,
A confetti of giggling little girls.
In the beginning it comes soft-flowing,
An otherness almost beyond knowing.

Leaves!
Nadine Luoma
Grand Rapids, Minnesota

Like pennies   at the wind's command
shaken from a bank, drop . . .
the leaves   one by one.

Autumn
Sheila Monether
Cheshire, England

Tell me about your golden road
Now that the leaves have gone.
Do branches pattern the evening sky
When day is almost done?
Are the leaves all faded now,
The red, the yellow, and brown?
Do they crunch beneath your feet
As you stamp them on the ground?
Are the cobwebs frosty?
Don't spoil their lacey thread.
Just huff your breath in a silent roar—
Make clouds around your head.
Remember, when you are cold or sad,
As you walk in the snow and rain,
That after winter, spring, and sun,
Your road will be golden again.

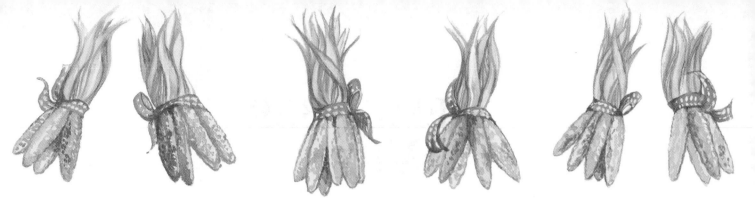

An Autumn Twilight

Rosemary Baker
LeClaire, Iowa

The tangerine moon
hangs low in the sky,
and the stars are reflecting
in a lake close by.

Echoes of loons
drift hauntingly clear,
as a chorus of frogs
harmonizes on a pier.

Shadows of deer
silhouette in the light,
while woodburning incense
lingers into the night.

A quietness prevails,
for tranquility is here;
days of autumn are to cherish
before they disappear.

November

Louise O'Brien
Colrain, Massachusetts

The sumacs' warm red torches
    Outline the leaden sky;
The white birch, slender, sways
    As the cold wind hurries by.

The muted roar of the river
    As it flings itself along
Seems a maiden with foam-flecked tresses
    Abandoning self to song.

So cold and gray are the rocks
    Where the green moss fails to creep;
The brown leaves litter the ground
    And are restless before they sleep.

The earth is a cold, gray monotone
    Waiting winter's arrival;
But a touch of color, of warmth, of life,
    Promise a sure survival.

Readers are invited to submit original poetry for possible publication in future issues of IDEALS. *Please send typed copies only; manuscripts will not be returned. Writers receive payment for each published submission. Send material to Readers' Reflections, Ideals Publications, 535 Metroplex Drive, Suite 250, Nashville, Tennessee 37211.*

REMEMBER WHEN

Gladys Taber

NOVEMBER

When the children come for Thanksgiving, out comes the big roaster. Dinner is traditional, including fluffy turnips, cranberry sauce, giblet gravy, mashed potatoes. We do not, however, have the mince and apple pies. This is a sign of the times, for the children count calories and prefer to use them up on the main dinner. The small ones have dishes of ice cream while the adults have a fruit bowl, cheese, and crackers.

Toward evening, everyone is ready for cold turkey and thinly sliced dressing for sandwiches. It is self-service, for Mama is through for the day! Later we get out the corn popper and a bowl of apples in case anyone is starving. We like corn popped in a rusty old popper from the early days, shaken back and forth over the embers in the fireplace. I use part oil and part butter and more salt than anyone would believe. My feeling is the oil spreads the butter more evenly—but this may be another of my notions.

I remember when turkey was a once-in-a-year dinner. It symbolized Thanksgiving. Ham was for Easter, along with eggs cooked in fancy ways. Roast beef and Yorkshire pudding meant Christmas in our house when I was growing up, or stuffed goose when Mama could get it.

Our turkey came to town from a farm near Black Creek, I believe, and I stood around waiting to see Father bring it in the house. Then that delicious smell of sage and onion and savory filled the house as Mama stuffed his majesty and tucked him in the gas oven (allowing plenty of time for the gas to die down around suppertime as it always did).

We were in Wisconsin and the relatives in New England, so a family gathering was out of

All the leaves were put in the big mahogany table and the great lace cloth laid on.

the question but Mama had a houseful, as usual—the family doctor and his wife, a couple of homesick students from the college, a couple of single members of the faculty. All the leaves were put in the big mahogany table and the great lace cloth laid on. Father always said a hurried gruff blessing, for it embarrassed him to talk publicly to God. He addressed Him in private rather as one equal to another, but at the dinner table he flushed and ran the words together.

Nowadays turkey is so available it is no longer a seasonal treat. At times I am sorry it is so common, for that first thrill of seeing it on Thanksgiving morning is gone. The grandchildren accept turkey as just another good meal. I won't go so far as to say it should be restricted to holidays, but a few things should still be rare treats, I think.

Thanksgiving dinner preparations begin in an organized kitchen. Photograph from SuperStock.

November for me is a good time for meditation. As I watch the violet twilight casting shadows over the valley, I think what a long way we have come since the post riders spurred their horses down from Boston and our church bell rang out and everyone gathered to hear the news of Concord and Lexington. It took, I believe, two days for word to reach here.

I am thankful for so very much. No voice is raised in hatred in my household. Footsteps sound gently on the threshold, with no echo of nailed boots. The grandchildren walk and play without fear. The dogs settle on the wide hearth and doze into a warm, comfortable sleep. The steady glow of friendship warms me daily: Joe brings me a new load of firewood; Erma takes me to the dentist in the next town so that I won't have to go alone; Steve and Wilma bring me some special country sausage, which they get from the South.

These are simple things, but to me they are most precious. And as I recall each one, November's beaver moon shines brighter than ever and I know that love and friendship, hearth fires, and faith are indeed gifts to be thankful for and to treasure always.

This selection appeared in STILLMEADOW CALENDAR, *published by J. P. Lippincott Company in 1967.*

GRAND DESIGN

Lucyann Murray

Autumn's days call out to us,
Their timbre crisp and clear.
In voice akin to music,
They warn us winter's near.

With golden foliage drifting,
Bright pumpkins on the vine,
Soon calm will be replaced
With storms that bend the pine.

We warm ourselves with cider
And walk through wooded land
To marvel at earth's canvas
God has drawn in His freehand.

Fall's colors tint the landscape,
An artist's holy shrine.
Blessed are we, held within
The good Lord's grand design.

A small cottage is reflected in a beaver pond in the Rangely Lakes Region of Maine. Photograph by William H. Johnson.

MIRRORED BEAUTY

Loise Pinkerton Fritz

Autumn is in the valley;
It dews the grass each morn;
It strolls among the meadows
And pastures, cattle-worn.

It skims across the cornfields
Where ripened cobs hang low;
It's seen in frost that sparkles
On pumpkins' ripe orange glow.

Autumn is on the hillsides;
It's in the forests too.
It's mirrored in the sunsets
And in the harvest moon.

Autumn in its beauty
Everywhere abounds;
If we look a little closer,
In our hearts it can be found.

33

A Robin's Song
Marvin H. Thompson

Amid bare trees a robin sings.
The leaves are shed, the summer's gone;
Yet in the frosty autumn air,
The songbird valiantly sings on.

The fields are bleak, his mates have flown,
The grain is reaped and stored away,
Naught to call forth his song, and still
His joyful music greets the day.

Eternal faith is in that song,
That spring will follow winter's cold,
When warmth shall bring a friendly throng
And food and gladness as of old.

I shall take courage from his faith,
That God, who marks the sparrow's flight,
Till spring tide floods my soul again
Will walk beside me through the night.

Heavenward
Dorothy B. Taggart

For those who sense the time the wild geese fly,
There is a sorrow on an autumn day.
They hear the leaving song across the sky,
A fugue, crescendoing from far away.

And high above the morning's silvery veil,
They sight the forceful leader of the wedge,
And white-cheeked followers who trail,
According to their place, along the edge.

So fast the squadron passes in its aim,
The counterpointed song fades on the air,
Trailing but the single leaving strain,
Like a "goodbye" to earthbound listening there.

At Siuslaw National Forest, Oregon, a vine maple displays its brilliant autumn foliage. Photograph by Terry Donnelly/Donnelly Austin Photography.

Nests in Autumn
Glenn Ward Dresbach

Under the shocks of grain,
    Field mice are warm today
In round nests that retain
    Soft, faded bits of summer.
    Someone will come tomorrow
And haul the grain away.

High in the golden tree,
    The squirrels' nest is gold,
Almost too bright to see
    Against the flood of sunlight.
    Bare boughs will show some morning
One nest against the cold.

What have you better than these,
    O Dreams, for a winter nest?
It is so in the fields, in the trees,
    When the bright harvests are over,
    When the golden leaves drift earthward.
It is so in this troubled breast.

To a Waterfowl

William Cullen Bryant

Whither, midst falling dew,
While glow the heavens with the last steps of day,
Far, through their rosy depths, dost thou pursue
    Thy solitary way?
    Vainly the fowler's eye
Might mark thy distant flight to do thee wrong,
As, darkly painted on the crimson sky,
    Thy figure floats along.

Seek'st thou the plashy brink
Of weedy lake, or marge of river wide,
Or where the rocking billows rise and sink
    On the chafed oceanside?

There is a Power whose care
Teaches thy way along that pathless coast—
The desert and illimitable air—
    Lone wandering, but not lost.

All day thy wings have fanned,
At that far height the cold, thin atmosphere,
Yet stop not, weary, to the welcome land,
    Though the dark night is near.

And soon that toil shall end;
Soon shalt thou find a summer home, and rest,
And scream among thy fellows; reeds shall bend,
    Soon, o'er thy sheltered nest.

Thou'rt gone, the abyss of heaven
Hath swallowed up thy form; yet on my heart
Deeply hath sunk the lesson thou hast given,
    And shall not soon depart:
    He who, from zone to zone,
Guides through the boundless sky thy certain flight,
In the long way that I must tread alone,
    Will lead my steps aright.

In a painting entitled AUTUMN'S BLESSINGS, Diane Phalen's
mallards fly past a serene yard with beautifully designed
quilts on display. Painting © Diane Phalen Watercolors.

Enchanted Days

Charles A. Brotzman

When the flocks are flying south
In form across the sky;
When the flowers bow their heads
To kiss the earth and die;

When the grapevine sags beneath
The burden it has grown;
When the days are golden bright
Before the leaves have flown;

When the plowman's cheery note
Is heard the field around;
When the fallen McIntosh
Lie thick upon the ground;

When the hills are set ablaze
In yellow, gold, and red;
When the corn shocks stand in line,
So lifelike although dead;

When the night air has a sting,
And distant sounds are clear;
When the sighing pine trees tell
That winter hovers near;

When the moonlight makes light as day
The countryside around;
And when the frosty shadows
Lie ghostly on the ground;

No other season has it,
That which I cannot name.
No other time awakens
A feeling quite the same.

Oh, then I have the yearning
To roam through wood and dell,
But I am lost completely
When held in Autumn's spell.

O Autumn, you enchant me;
My soul is not my own.
Your beauty calls and calls me
In nature's richest tones.

Oh, I could sit for hours
And drink your beauty in;
But I am drunk with rapture
Almost before I begin.

Give me the season Autumn,
The climax to the year,
Nature's grand finale,
When Autumn's days are here.

Bond Falls, on the Ontonagon River in Ontonagon County, Michigan, is framed by the dramatic colors of autumn leaves. Photograph by Darryl R. Beers.

Autumn Cheer

Kay Hoffman

I like the golden autumn days,
The fruited vine, the bluish haze,
The stillness along the country way,
Sweet fragrance of the new-mown hay.

I like to see wild geese in flight,
Especially on a moonlit night,
The smell of apple-scented breeze,
Sunlight flickering through colored leaves.

I like to walk the leaf-bright trails,
Watch sunset lift flame, red-gold sails.
Of all the seasons of the year,
I like the smile of autumn cheer.

October Observer

Charlotte Partin

A chilling wind rustles,
Underneath
Thistles.
Up in a tree,
Mistletoe
Nestles!

October

George R. Kossik

The leaves were bright and beautiful
With hues of gold and flame;
October decked the hills and vales
With glory when she came.

At close of day when sunset shone
Above the farthest hill,
The sight was such that I would stare
In contemplation still.

Serene with splendor, beauty bright,
Yet soon the leaves would fall;
But in my heart I'll never forget
The wonder of it all.

*An old ivy-draped tree guards the entrance
to Cherokee Park, Louisville, Kentucky.
Photograph by Daniel E. Dempster.*

At the Farm

E. K. Haarstad

Though the autumn breeze had chilled us,
The bright sunshine kept us warm
As we brought the garden produce
To the cellar on the farm.

Pails of freshly dug potatoes
Were piled on the earthen floor.
Nubby squash and yellow pumpkins
Had their corner by the door.

Apples packed in bushel baskets,
Carrots in a box of sand,
Several heads of crispy cabbage—
All were riches of our land.

Rows of peaches, pears, and berries
In glass jars upon the shelves,
Cans of corn and red tomatoes
Had been processed by ourselves.

Weary, tired, but contented,
We walked through the kitchen door.
Rich aromas from the cookstove
Told us supper was in store.

Oh, our hearts were overflowing
And we felt an inner glow
As we thanked our God for blessings
On the farm so long ago.

In The Gathering, *artist Bob Pettes depicts
several generations of family members arriving
at Grandmother's house for Thanksgiving
dinner. Painting © Bob Pettes.*

Mom's Pumpkin Pie

Phyllis C. Michael

Pumpkin pie, Mom's pumpkin pie—
The kind she used to bake!
Oh, how I wish I had a piece,
Just for old times' sake.
To be sure, my waistline doesn't need pie,
Not even one small slice;
But pumpkin pie, Mom's pumpkin pie,
Was really very nice.

It came from pumpkins we had raised
Out there in the fields of corn;
We boys and Dad used to haul them in
On our wagon, now old and worn.
The kitchen used to smell of spice
On a chilly autumn day
When we came in, we boys, from chores,
Or from our game or play.

Pumpkin pie, Mom's pumpkin pie!
I can see it sitting there
On the kitchen sink, just to cool a bit—
How I wish I now had my share.

Thanksgiving Time

Author Unknown

When all the leaves are off the boughs,
And nuts and apples gathered in,
And cornstalks waiting for the cows,
And pumpkins safe in barn and bin;

Then Mother says: "My children dear,
The fields are brown, and Autumn flies;
Thanksgiving Day is very near,
And we must make Thanksgiving pies!"

The lawn of Peckham Farm, Pownal, Vermont, is stacked with harvest pumpkins and beautiful chrysanthemums. Photograph by Dick Dietrich/Dietrich Leis Stock Photography.

FROM MY GARDEN JOURNAL

Lisa Ragan

BUTTERNUT SQUASH

As Thanksgiving rolls around each year, I often find myself wondering just what was served at that first Thanksgiving table. Many have theorized about the various foods, but one vegetable was almost certainly present—squash. And due to the nature of squash to keep fresh for long periods, the butternut squash may have been the one of choice for those first Pilgrims and their Native American friends.

AN AMERICAN ORIGINAL

Historians have surmised that the squash likely originated in Central and South America and then was gradually cultivated farther and farther north.

Underscoring its centuries-old popularity is the fact that squash seeds have even been found in ancient Mexican burial caves. When Europeans arrived in the New World, Native Americans were already cultivating the squash, and it was soon adopted by the new settlers.

A HARD-SHELLED BEAUTY

The butternut squash plant produces a tan-colored fruit with a long, thick neck which brings to mind an overgrown pear. Inside the hard shell, the nutritious butternut yields pumpkin-colored flesh with especially high concentrations of Vitamin C and beta carotene. The small seed cavity sits at the bottom of the squash, taking up little room. The plant itself produces a vigorous vine with hairy leaves and big blossoms, although some varieties produce semibush plant forms.

A LITTLE VARIETY

Among the butternut cultivars and varieties, the Waltham strain stands out as a popular favorite. The Waltham butternut grows on aggressive vines and yields a three- to six-pound fruit with rich, sweet, dry flesh with excellent flavor and aroma. For those gardeners who prefer a semi-

BUTTERNUT SQUASH

bush plant, the Early Butternut hybrid is a semi-bush form that has developed a reputation as a great producer of fruits with good flavor. Two other prolific varieties include Ponca Butter, an early producer of small fruits, and the Zenith Hybrid, which yields small, heavy fruits.

MY, HOW YOU'VE GROWN

Butternut squash can be grown from seed or transplants. Once the soil has warmed sufficiently in late spring, seeds should be sown in a location that receives eight hours of full sun, ideally, but at least four to six hours of full sun per day. In areas with especially hot summers, squash vines may prefer a little afternoon shade.

PLANTING AND NURTURING

Plant seeds in mounds of rich, well-drained soil about six inches high and eighteen inches in diameter. Begin with five seeds per mound, or hill, as they are sometimes called, nurturing to maturity only the best one or two seedlings. Winter squashes are thirsty and hungry plants that require steady water and heavy mulch. Butternuts will forgive a dry spell, however, and recover fully.

A HARVEST OF RICHES

Squash vines need plenty of room to sprawl unless they are trained up a trellis, fence, or post. If allowed to lie on the ground, the fruits can be protected if cushioned with newspapers or straw. The plants require more than ninety days to reach maturity and will appreciate an application of phosphorus after three weeks of growth. For the best taste and texture, the gardener should thin each squash plant to three or four fruits.

Butternut squashes cannot be picked from the vine and brought indoors to ripen like a tomato. The fruits must mature fully on the vine and can be harvested when the shell resists being punctured with a fingernail. Harvesting must be completed before frost, and any fruits that get frostbitten should go to the compost pile.

THE PICTURE OF HEALTH

Of all the types of squash, the hardy butternut squash resists the most pests and diseases. In fact, the solid stems of the butternut squash easily thwart squash borers. Some gardeners always plant basil with squash to protect the squash from the mildew that can grow at harvest time in areas with cool or damp autumns.

Butternut is such an easy winter squash to cultivate that even the novice vegetable gardener can grow a lovely vine that produces a bounty of delicious fruit and then serve it to family and friends come November. ❧

The Pilgrims likely gave thanks not only for their new Native American friends but also for a wholly American vegetable, the butternut squash. And as we celebrate the holiday today, we should also be thankful that we have this delicious and hardy addition to our Thanksgiving dinner choices.

Lisa Ragan tends a small but mighty garden in Nashville, Tennessee, with the help of her son, Trenton.

FAMILY RECIPES

CRESCENT APPLE DESSERT

Barbara Bevis, Newbern, Tennessee

2 large Granny Smith apples
2 8-ounce cans crescent
   roll dough
1 cup orange juice
1/2 cup butter
1 cup granulated sugar

Preheat oven to 350°F. Peel, core, and cut apples into eighths. Separate crescent roll dough into 16 triangles. Wrap one apple slice in each piece of dough, starting at shortest side of triangle and rolling to opposite point. Arrange in a greased, 9-by-13-inch pan with point side down. In a medium saucepan, combine orange juice, butter, and sugar; heat until sugar is dissolved and butter is melted, stirring well. Pour over rolls. Bake 25 minutes or until golden brown. Serve warm. Makes 16 servings.

APPLE-SQUASH CASSEROLE

Beth Christman, Boyertown, Pennsylvania

1/2 cup light brown sugar
1 tablespoon all-purpose flour
1 teaspoon salt
1/2 teaspoon ground mace
1/4 cup butter, melted
2 pounds butternut squash, peeled,
   seeded, and cut into small chunks
2 large apples, cored and cut into
   1/2-inch slices

Preheat oven to 350°F. In a medium bowl, combine brown sugar, flour, salt, and mace. Add butter, mixing well. In an ungreased, 9-by-13-inch pan, arrange squash. Top with apple slices; spread with sugar mixture. Cover and bake 60 minutes, until squash is tender. Makes 8 servings.

COUNTRY BAKED APPLES

Edmona Lohr, Minonk, Illinois

1 cup sweet apple cider
½ cup granulated sugar
2 tablespoons butter
¼ teaspoon cinnamon

1 tablespoon cornstarch
⅛ teaspoon salt
6 baking apples, peeled, cored,
   and cut into chunks

Preheat oven to 350°F. In a large saucepan, combine cider, sugar, butter, cinnamon, cornstarch, and salt; cook over medium heat until boiling. Carefully stir in apple chunks. Spread apple mixture in a greased, 9-by-13-inch baking dish. Bake 60 minutes or until apples are tender. Serve warm with a scoop of vanilla ice cream. Makes 8 servings.

THANKSGIVING BAKE

Amy Dietrick, Gilbertsville, Pennsylvania

3 sweet potatoes, peeled and quartered
1 cup brown sugar, divided
1 teaspoon cinnamon
1 teaspoon ground nutmeg

2 large cooking apples, peeled, cored,
   quartered, and cut into ¼-inch slices
¼ cup all-purpose flour
¼ cup butter, cut into small pieces
½ cup chopped pecans

Preheat oven to 350°F. In a large saucepan, boil sweet potatoes 25 minutes or until tender. Drain, cool, and cut into ¼-inch slices. In a small bowl, mix ½ cup brown sugar with cinnamon and nutmeg. Layer sweet potatoes, sugar mixture, and apples in a greased, 7-by-11-inch baking dish. In a medium bowl, mix flour, butter, remaining brown sugar, and pecans, until mixture crumbles. Sprinkle over potatoes and apples. Bake 30 minutes or until lightly browned. Makes 8 servings.

Add color and new flavors to your Thanksgiving table with these vegetable and apple recipes. We would love to share your favorite recipe too. Send a typed copy to Ideals Publications, 535 Metroplex Drive, Nashville, Tennessee 37211. Payment will be provided for each recipe published.

Apple Butter Making

Nora G. Gillespie

Apples are in the orchard,
Juicy, ripe, and sweet,
Willin' folks to pick them,
To sneak some to eat.
Cider is awaitin'
Hands to peel; don't tarry.
Throw a whole peel over shoulders
To see whom you will marry.
Scrub the old brass kettle;
Wooden stirrer must be clean;
Gather wood for fire—
What a busy scene!

Add the sugar as it cooks
And at last the spice to taste;
Have the clean jars ready,
Not a drop to waste.
Now the goodness thickens;
The scent is in the air;
Everybody wants to taste,
Afraid he'll lose his share.
Arms grow tired from stirrin',
But then glad voices ring,
For with butter and hot biscuits,
It's eatin' fit for a king!

At Apple-Parin' Time

Phyllis C. Michael

When the year's at apple-parin' time
And the frost lies on the ground,
Then my thoughts go back, yes, a good piece back,
When old friends were all around.
My thoughts go back to a cozy room
Where the stove was shiny and black,
Where chairs were plain and worn and old,
But where love felt no sense of lack.

When the year's at apple-parin' time,
I see those chairs all filled—
There was Mom, Aunt Bess, and little Mae,
And love flowed so free that it spilled
From each face and it seemed to adorn the room,
Like gold in that lamplit place.
All fingers flew as they pared and cored
Those Winesaps as if in a race.

When the year's at apple-parin' time,
I feel the crisp, cool air;
I see the bonfire out by the barn
And two huge, black kettles there.
The men brought wood or sat and stirred
Around the welcome fire
Until the apple butter boiled up thick,
According to their desire.

When the year's at apple-parin' time,
I think about these things
And wish that I were there again
With all the joys it would bring.
I think about, well, this and that,
And wish that kids today
Could go to just one apple bee
In the same old-fashioned way.

*Lush varieties of apples harvested in Willamette Valley,
Oregon, appear irresistible. Photograph by Steve Terrill.*

Apple-Happy

Beverly McLoughland

The smell of
apple pie
baking
in the oven
drifts through the
house
on long, invisible
ribbons
of apple,
nutmeg,
and cinnamon—
leads us all
out of our rooms,
apple-happy
and dancing
round the warm
Maypole
kitchen.

Apple Time

Virginia Blanck Moore

It's apple time, and under trees
Bowed down with globes of red,
The fruit lies crimson as the dawn
Upon a green-grass bed.

It's apple time, and every bite
Is crisp and tangy-sweet,
A joy to every passerby
Who pauses there to eat.

It's apple time, ripe apple time,
And the harvester knows now
What miracles of taste can come
From sun and rain and bough.

Apples in a bowl make the perfect fall centerpiece in this painting by Isy Ochoa, entitled Sub Rosa. *Image from SuperStock.*

53

SLICE OF LIFE

Edna Jaques

THANKFUL

Not for the mighty world, O Lord, tonight,
    Nations and kingdoms in their fearful might,
Let me be glad the kettle gently sings,
    Let us be thankful just for little things.

Thankful for simple food and supper spread,
    Thankful for shelter and a warm, clean bed,
For little joyful feet that gladly run
    To welcome me when the day's work is done.

Thankful for friends who share my joy and mirth.
    Glad for the warm, sweet fragrance of the earth,
For golden pools of sunlight on the floor,
    For peace that bends above my cottage door.

For little friendly days that slip away
    With only meals and bed and work and play,
A rocking chair and kindly firelight—
    For little things, let us be glad tonight.

These young harvesters have as much fun picking apples as eating them. NOTHING LIKE JONATHANS © Robert Duncan. Image provided by Robert Duncan Studios.

Autumn Bliss

Joan Donaldson

The hazy autumn sunlight filtering through golden sassafras leaves illuminated our afternoon. The day before, my husband, John, and I had picked Red Delicious, McIntosh, and Jonathan apples, plus a few other personal favorites that John had selected for their unique flavor. The crates of apples circled our small family cider press like a garnet necklace. The air was as crisp as the apples and filled with their fragrance.

We had convinced friends from church to stop by and lend their muscles. Taking turns cranking the chopper, we all fed apples into the hopper. The pomace dropped into a net bag arranged in a wooden hoop. Above the rumble and whir of the blades as they sliced apples, folks commented about the tawny reds and golds of the hardwoods west of our clover field.

A flock of sandhill cranes wheeled overhead, reminding us of the approaching winter months. Only a few more mellow afternoons would grace the fall before snowstorms swept across Lake Michigan and our farm. It was high time to fill our root cellar with rows of winter squash, plus bushels of potatoes and apples.

Even before the hoop was filled with ground apples, juice trickled between the slats and yellow jackets hovered about the area. When the net bag was full, John placed a circle of wood on top of it and turned the overhead screw. The amber liquid gushed through the slats, over the platform, and into a waiting jug. Each twist of the crank increased the flow until finally the apple pomace had yielded all its juice. Cups were filled, and, like judges at the county fair, we sipped and breathed in the bouquet of fresh cider.

"Maybe it needs a few more Red Delicious apples?" John asked. "Or is it sweet enough?" Ever the connoisseur, my husband likes his cider on the sweet side and works for the best blend of apples.

"Perhaps a few more Delicious," I replied, while tucking away a few Jonagolds for apple crisp. The best of this variety will be stored in our cave-like root cellar. John's favorite evening treat in the winter is a peeled Jonagold, still sweet and crunchy.

Helping hands emptied the pomace into buckets. Once again the whir of the blades slowed as apples were tossed into the hopper. Friends cranked the press and filled jars to take home. Our own jugs were full and would be set in the freezer tonight. During this winter, we would share the cider at potlucks and dinner parties.

The lengthening shadows, empty crates, and the cries of the geese headed towards the river hinted that chore time drew near. Gracie, one of the barn cats, sat in the loft window of the goat barn, watching and waiting. The chickens cackled their approval when a couple of us dumped the pomace into their pen. Such a succulent treat would reward us with more eggs tomorrow. Friends collected jackets and sweaters while John hosed down the cider press and carried it to the barn. We hoped that we would have one more mild afternoon when we would repeat this process.

We hugged our friends goodbye and they hopped into their cars, cradling their jars of cider. We hoped that each sip they took during the week would taste not only of fall's bounty, but also of the joy shared on that golden afternoon.

An old-fashioned country kitchen awaits holiday preparations. Photograph by Jessie Walker.

For Crows and Jays

Beverly McLoughland

I sing a song
Of thanks and praise
For cranky crows
And feisty jays,
Who could have lived
A life of ease
Sailing on a southern breeze
But gave up warm and

Sunny skies
To stay behind and
Criticize
November's damp
And bitter cold
With squawk, and
Bellyache, and
Scold.

First Monday of November

Mary Lou Carney

How did all the leaves know to fall today,
    the first Monday of November?
In one crusty night of forty-degree rain,
    the brittle beauty of October is gone.
Branches stretch empty hands
    toward skies that darken too early.
I drag my rusty rake through piles of leaves,
    mound them into mountains of soggy brown.
A gray squirrel chatters down at me from a nearby tree.
He runs round and round the trunk,
    like the endlessly moving
    stripes on a barber's pole.
Then,
with a flamboyant flash of his furry tail,
friend-squirrel scurries off
to scavenge for winter nuts—
leaving me leaning on the handle of my rake
determining the things I should
"store up" for coming months:
    the warmth of August afternoons,
    a little July sunshine,
    the gentleness of full-moon October nights,
    and the optimism of a March crocus.

Fall harvest produce and fresh flowers offer a bright tapestry of the season's treasures. Photograph by Larry LeFever/Grant Heilman.

HANDMADE HEIRLOOM

Melissa Lester

GOURD BIRD FEEDERS

When her youngest child left home, my mother accepted her empty nest by turning her attention outward—outdoors, that is. Among the new pursuits she finally had time to explore, she took up bird watching. A bird feeder suspended outside her kitchen window brought many feathered friends into her backyard. Mother kept a reference book on the kitchen counter to help her quickly identify new visitors to the feeder.

Making a bird feeder is a pleasant way to open the door to this new hobby, and a hard-shell gourd is a natural choice for such a project. Gourds hold the distinction of being the only plant grown all over the world. Their cultivation can be traced back thousands of years in China and other countries around the globe. Dried gourds are water-resistant and buoyant, so some archaeologists believe that gourds floated across the seas and crashed against rocks, breaking their woodlike shells and spilling seeds on distant shores.

Gourds are too bitter to eat, but their design makes them perfect for utilitarian purposes. As a gourd matures on the vine, its stem cuts off the flow of nutrients. As it dries in the sun, it develops a hard shell which protects the seeds inside. Artifacts indicate that gourds have been used in a variety of ways. They have been employed in many cultures to store wet and dry

goods, and they have also been used to make musical instruments, flotation devices, and armor. Gourds were even used as currency at one time in Haiti.

Gourds are commonly used as bird feeders today. The Amish use feeders in their fields to attract colonies of purple martins to help keep crops insect-free. Recreational gardeners use the feeders because they appreciate the gourd's form or enjoy observing the birds they attract. Dried

---

A gourd feeder can be a wonderful way to invite serenity into your life.

---

gourds purchased from farms allow crafters to make bird feeders with ease, perhaps as a family or classroom project. Among the gourd varieties are dipper, penguin, martin, birdhouse, and Chinese.

The first step in making a gourd bird feeder is to wash the gourd with a scouring pad and a mild soap solution. This will remove the gourd's thin outer shell to reveal its underlying pale yellow to dark brown color. The easiest way to create an entrance hole for the feeder is with a hole saw, but a circle can be drawn by hand and cut out with a small hacksaw. The edge of the entrance hole should then be sanded smooth.

The next step is to remove the pulp and seeds from the inside of the gourd. A long-handled spoon should work well to scrape the inside walls and pull out the matter. Material pulled from the gourd can be discarded or saved to be put back in the feeder to provide nesting material for the birds.

At this point, several small holes need to be drilled in the top and bottom of the feeder. Two holes drilled through the top can be wired for hanging the completed feeder, while four holes drilled in the bottom of the gourd will allow for drainage.

The shell of the gourd can be left plain to let its natural beauty shine through, or the bird feeder can be embellished with a wood-burning tool, waterproof pens, acrylic paints, or leather dye. The outside of the gourd should stand up well to the elements, but a coat of linseed oil, shoe polish, or polyurethane applied to the shell will provide extra protection. The feeder will last longer if stored inside during the winter and coated with a protective finish each year.

The completed bird feeder can be hung using a piece of copper wire threaded through the two holes drilled in the top of the gourd. Hung in an open field, the feeder may attract eastern bluebirds, northern flickers, purple martins, and swallows. Placing the feeder near the house will more likely attract wrens, chickadees, downy woodpeckers, or house finches. As the final step, birdseed placed inside the feeder will invite birds to come calling.

Along with a variety of feathered friends, a gourd bird feeder can be a wonderful way to invite serenity into your life. During my

Dried gourds may be decorated, stained, painted, or left natural to add interest to your outdoor garden. Gourds cultivated and handcrafted at Bluebird Meadows, Stevensville, Michigan. Photograph by Gerald Koser.

mother's first days with an empty nest, she missed the day-to-day contact with her three children. Concerns for our future and well-being filled her mind; yet somehow, watching birds visit her feeder brought comfort. Watching them feed and frolic, Mother was reminded of Matthew 6:26: "Behold the fowls of the air: for they sow not, neither do they reap, nor gather into barns; yet your heavenly Father feedeth them. Are ye not much better than they?" Realizing that she had given her children wings and that we could never move beyond our Father's love, Mother's spirit, like the birds in her feeder, was able to take flight.

Melissa Lester is a freelance writer living in Wetumpka, Alabama, with her husband, two sons, and a daughter. She contributes to a number of magazines and authored the book GIVING FOR ALL IT'S WORTH.

FOR THE CHILDREN

Thanksgiving Blessings

Eileen Spinelli

Bless the meadows.
Bless the deer.
Bless our loved ones,
   far and near.

Bless the apple-
   scented air.
Bless the food
   that we prepare.

Bless the beaches.
Bless the birds.
Bless the tender
   shapes of words.

Bless the cities.
Bless the geese.
Bless the fragile
   wings of peace.

Bless the mountains.
Bless the streams.
Bless our starry,
   borrowed dreams.

Bless the moon
And bless the sheep
And bless the stranger,
   sound asleep.

This painting by Charles Burton (1845–1894) is appropriately entitled SUSPENSE as two pets await the optimal moment for grabbing a precious treat. Image provided by Fine Art Photographic Library.

DEVOTIONS FROM THE HEART

Pamela Kennedy

I thank my God every time I remember you. —*Philippians 1:3* (NIV)

THANKS FOR THE MEMORIES

For years our furniture was what I like to call "eclectic." It sounds so much more elegant than "mismatched." My husband's Navy career spanned twenty-eight years and included eighteen moves. I never felt it was very wise to invest in expensive, coordinated furnishings that would be packed by burly men into moving vans every so often and transported thousands of miles across land and sea. So we picked up a kitchen set at the Veteran's Thrift Store, bought a secretary desk at a garage sale, made a dining room table from an old ship's hatch cover, gave refuge to many of our neighbors' castoffs, and liberated odds and ends from our parents' basements.

At one point, however, I remember wishing for a nice china cabinet to hold some of my special belongings. So when I found a beautiful reproduction of an antique oak cabinet through an ad in the paper, I decided to purchase it. I admitted it was a risk, but, amazingly, the beveled glass and carved wood never endured a crack or scratch, despite being moved across the continent four times and making two round trips between Hawaii and the mainland!

If you've ever moved, you know that unpacking can be a tedious and wearing task.

There are never enough of the right-sized spaces for what you've brought, and the empty boxes and packing paper threaten to take over your new dwelling. Moving in tested tempers and I never looked forward to it. But filling the china cabinet was different. I saved it for last and then savored the experience.

Every time I unwrapped and replaced the different items on the oak and glass shelves, it

---

Thank You, Lord, for the rich memories of those who have lived before me and blessed me with a heritage of family and faith.

---

was like welcoming my extended family into my new home. There is a small cream pitcher from the 1904 World's Fair in St. Louis, with "Lillie Dalrymple," the name of my maternal great-grandmother, etched into its cranberry coating. Behind the pitcher are hand-painted salt and pepper shakers from Prussia, a wedding gift to my parents over sixty years ago. My own wedding china gleams in ivory and platinum next to a primitive wood carving of a cow whittled by a great uncle during the First World War. My children's baby teeth rest in a silver sugar bowl that once graced the table of my husband's grandmother. An elegant chocolate pot from an aunt and a small lead soldier that belonged to my father rest side by side on a shelf above Grandma's antique crystal cruet set. It's a hodgepodge of items—eclectic, one might say—but together they make up the memories of a family.

I never knew many of the relatives whose treasures I now own. And several that I did know I will never see again. But I can hold these belongings of theirs, run my fingers along the cool edges of cut crystal or the rough wood of a carving, and somehow feel connected to the men and women in my family tree.

When the Apostle Paul penned the words "I thank my God every time I remember you," I think I know how he may have felt. It is often easy to feel alone and separated from those we love, but each of us has a heritage of family and faith that fills our hearts with memories. Sometimes those memories are firsthand; at other times they are passed along through family stories or special mementos. However they come to us, these memories are gifts of love drawing us ever tighter into the family circle.

As we gather around the Thanksgiving table and offer thanks for our present blessings, it is good to also be grateful for those who have filled our hearts with special memories from generations past.

A traditional Thanksgiving feast awaits a family. Photograph by Jessie Walker.

Pamela Kennedy is a freelance writer of short stories, articles, essays, and children's books. Wife of a retired naval officer and mother of three children, she has made her home on both U.S. coasts and currently resides in Honolulu, Hawaii.

Give Thanks

LaVeta Stankavich

For scarlet flame of maple tree,
The gold and black of velvet bee,
A sunset's mauve infinity,
    For all of these, give thanks.

For southbound geese with haunting cry,
A bobwhite's whistled, clear reply,
The night wind's plaintive lullaby,
    For all of these, give thanks.

For rich, redolent, roadside mint,
Belated Concords' heady scent,
Bread's fresh-baked, fragrant nourishment,
    For all of these, give thanks.

A Thankful Heart

Garnett Ann Schultz

Oh, let me know a thankful heart,
A heart where love doth dwell,
Where hope and faith and lasting peace
Are known and treasured well,
An ever-understanding heart,
A strength so real and sure,
A heart that ever looks to God
To strengthen and endure.

Oh, give me a thankful heart,
That I may live each day
As though tomorrow shall not come,
No thought of yesterday—
A thankfulness for what I have,
However large or small;
Just let me know a joy complete
To live and last through all.

God, grant I have a thankful heart
For blessings rich and true,
That I shall still accept my lot
With wants and wishes few.
The world is mine with all it brings,
Each lovely day so rare;
Just let me know it's still enough
That You are ever there.

I still must keep a thankful heart,
As years will hurry by,
To know a loveliness more real
That ever lights my eye;
The richest blessing life can send,
With treasures to impart—
It's this I ask for evermore—
A truly thankful heart.

These Zinfandel grapes are natural art on a vine. Photograph by Christi Carter/Grant Heilman.

Remembering Blessings

Shirley Sallay

There is a crispness at this time
Refreshing to behold;
Evening comes quite early
With sunset's tinge of gold.
The holy days are close at hand,
Excitement fills the air,
And talk of family gatherings
Is heard most everywhere.
So it is only proper
We pause a bit to pray
And give our thanks for blessings
Upon this festive day.
Think back across the year behind;
Recall each precious gift;
Then let the words of thankful praise
Your grateful heart uplift.

Though Our Mouths Were Full of Song

Author Unknown

Though our mouths were full of song as the sea,
and our tongues of exultation as the multitude of its waves,
and our lips of praise as the wide-extended firmament;
though our eyes shone with light like the sun and the moon,
and our hands were spread forth like the eagles of heaven,
and our feet were swift as hinds,
we should still be unable to thank Thee and bless Thy name,
O Lord our God and God of our fathers,
for one thousandth or one ten-thousandth part
of the bounties which Thou hast bestowed
upon our fathers and upon us.

*Pilgrims humbly offer thanks in this painting
entitled* Pilgrims: Thanksgiving Dinner,
by William Van Doren. Image from SuperStock.

68

A Thanksgiving Hymn

Inez Marrs

Hear a thousand voices singing
Hymns of thanks to God above,
For a thousand hearts are filled
This day with gratitude and love.

For this land we love and cherish,
Where men sow and reap in peace,
Where every man can choose his faith,
And freedom shall not cease;

For the legacy of children;
For neighbors and loyal friends;
For work and hope and happiness;
For home and rest when each day ends;

For the joys the past has brought us
And can never take away;
For memories of loved ones gone
And company of those present today;

For ears to hear the song of birds;
For eyes to behold the flowers;
For all of nature's beauty
In this enchanted world of ours;

For abundance that surrounds us;
For life, health, and generous food;
For these things and many more,
We offer now our gratitude.

Thanksgiving

Elizabeth C. Libbey

Autumn comes in
With many joys:
Bright red berries,
Leaves all a-scatter,
Woodsmoke in the wind,
Schoolchildren's chatter,
The first gentle snowfall,
A cup of hot cider,
That good feeling of thanks
For the things small and grand
That sustain us together
In this blessed land.

Everyday Treasures

Beryl Halinbourg

Whatever powers there be, I have no creed
Of lore or ritual to shape my days,
But, to the bounty that fulfills my need,
My spirit sings in gratitude and praise

For home and peace; the warm companionship
Of faces known and loved throughout the years;
The small and unexpected joys that grip
The memory, the gesture that endears;

For shared achievement and the sweet content
Of books to calm and music to inspire;
For hours of pleasure in a garden spent;
The cat or dog asleep before the fire;

For all the beatitude that comes my way
And wears the simple garb of everyday.

A red barn with twin silos is beautifully framed by fall foliage. Photograph by William H. Johnson.

Pamela Kennedy

AN AUTHENTIC THANKSGIVING

Not so long ago, I thought it would be a fine idea to have a really authentic Thanksgiving. It would be just like that first Thanksgiving, with all the wonderful things we have come to love and cherish as traditional.

My husband wasn't really geared up for my foray into the past, but suggested that the tradition of Thanksgiving-day football probably had its roots in the original holiday and should, therefore, be perpetuated at our annual event as well. I was pretty sure the Pilgrims and Indians didn't toss around the pigskin, but I told him I'd check. So I set out on my quest to re-create that first memorable Thanksgiving feast celebrated by our stalwart Pilgrim ancestors almost four centuries ago.

My initial discovery was that the first Thanksgiving really wasn't. It was a Harvest Feast all right, but, when the conservative Protestant Pilgrims talked about thanksgiving, they meant a religious time of fasting and prayer. That big feast they had in 1621 was more of a celebration that they had survived the first year and an acknowledgement that they had God to thank for it. And the idea that the Pilgrims fixed dinner for a few visiting Indians was not quite right either. The real story is that there were almost twice as many Native Americans as Pilgrims and the Wampanoags brought most of the food! According to the accounts of the event written by Governor William Bradford, several of the Pilgrim men pro-vided wild ducks and geese they had shot, but it was the Indian hunters who brought along five deer to feed the crowd. In case you were wondering about mashed potatoes and gravy, you can forget that too. Potatoes had only recently been "discovered" by the English, and most of them still considered the tubers poisonous. They did have pumpkins, but not

---

The longer my research continued, the shorter my menu became.

---

the big, fat, orange kind we have today, and certainly no pies. Their flour had run out and there was no milk, cows being conspicuously absent from Plymouth. They did have an abundance of fish, however, along with eels, lobster, and clams. I didn't have to wonder what my family would think about sitting down to a feast of savory Thanksgiving eels. Cranberries were few and far between too, and fresh veggies were limited to watercress, boiled squash, and beans. No fluffy Parker House rolls either—just some fried bread made from ground corn.

The longer my research continued, the shorter my menu became. And then I made a most interesting discovery. By the time of this harvest feast—most likely in early fall of 1621—there were only four adult women left in the Pilgrim band. That meant that at this feast for fifty English settlers and ninety Indians, the menfolk must have helped with

Original artwork by Elaine Garvin.

the cooking. The menu might be disappointing, but this new wrinkle in the meal preparation cheered me right up.

That is until I found out that the feast wasn't just a Thursday afternoon event. It appears the festivities continued for three days. This gives the term "leftovers" a whole new meaning! What do you do with 150 guests that just won't leave? Well, it seems my husband was right. They played sports. Of course it wasn't a hotly contested football game between the Lions and the Packers, but there were sharp-shooting contests with arrows and muskets, some ball games and a footrace or two.

With every new discovery, I became more disenchanted. Pilgrims didn't dress all in black and there were no starched white collars and certainly no damask cloths on long wooden tables lined with chairs. And it wasn't even in November! I was flirting with serious disillusionment when I stumbled upon something else I didn't expect. This harvest celebration wasn't an idea unique to the Plymouth Pilgrims. The Native Americans had long celebrated the ingathering of their crops with feasts. This was a cultural occasion crossing lines of race and religion. The tradition of Thanksgiving was tied neither to recipes nor specific activities, but to the common spirit of humanity that longs to express gratitude to the One who provides and protects.

And that's when I realized that my Thanksgiving could be authentic after all. So I roasted my turkey and mashed my potatoes. I simmered my gravy, smothered my sweet potatoes in brown sugar, gelled my cranberries, and baked my pumpkin pies. And when we sat down to dinner, just as our ancestors have done for hundreds of years, we joined hands and thanked our Creator for the blessings of provision and protection. We laughed and reminisced about good friends and favorite family memories.

And when the meal had ended, while the women cleaned up the kitchen and packed away tasty leftovers, our male Pilgrims and braves gathered around the glow of the television to celebrate the traditional conclusion of any authentic Thanksgiving—a sporting contest between two worthy opponents!

Thankfulness

Johnielu Barber Bradford

Our thanks to God can be so many things:
A grateful pause to note a rose at dawn,
A listening moment when a cardinal sings.
Or thanks can be a smile when day is gone,
A silent prayer, or eyes that gaze afar
In humbleness at all creation's spread,
Or gladness in the heart for every star.
How often when the Holy Word is read
And meditations follow, calm and sweet,
The spirit yields unuttered thanks for life
And for communion at the Master's feet,
For peace and beauty in a world of strife.
Our thankfulness to God is any move
Whereby we turn to Him with thoughts of love.

Gratitude

E. A. M. Moore

For leaves that glow in blazing destiny
Against the sapphire of the autumn sky,
For each breathtaking cosmic mystery,
For friends that grow more dear as time goes by—
Our thanks for these. And thanks for so much more:
For books and music, and the joys they bring,
For wit and repartee and wisdom's store,
For all the good we see in everything,
For strength to bear the suffering time sends,
For guidance through emotions' torturing shoals,
For Your forgiving grace that heals and mends
The ravages that care brings to our souls—
We thank You, Lord, and pray that we may share
Your light and joy with others everywhere.

This cove is the perfect place for an afternoon row on Highland Lake, in Maine. Photograph by Dick Dietrich/Dietrich Leis Stock Photography.

Jonathan Edwards

FROM PERSONAL NARRATIVE

I had then, and at other times, the greatest delight in the holy Scriptures, of any book whatsoever. Oftentimes in reading it, every word seemed to touch my heart. I felt a harmony between something in my heart and those sweet and powerful words. I seemed often to see so much light exhibited by every sentence, and such a refreshing ravishing food communicated, that I could not get along in reading. Used oftentimes to dwell long on one sentence, to see the wonders contained in it; and yet almost every sentence seemed to be full of wonders.

I have loved the doctrines of the gospel; they have been to my soul like green pastures. The gospel has seemed to me to be the richest treasure, the treasure that I have most desired and longed that it might dwell richly in me. The way of salvation by Christ has appeared in a general way glorious and excellent, and most pleasant and beautiful.

Sugar maples surround the steeple at a New England meeting house in Ashfield, Maine. Photograph by William H. Johnson.

LEGENDARY AMERICANS

Doug Kennedy and Maud Dawson

JONATHAN EDWARDS

Jonathan Edwards's influence on Protestant religion in America has been profound. This Puritan Calvinist, for twenty-four years minister of one of the larger early American churches in Massachusetts, has been described by more than one historian as America's greatest theologian. He is also the author and preacher of the most famous sermon ever written in English, "Sinners in the Hands of an Angry God." His various writings are still being read and studied by theologians, philosophers, historians, and Christians of many faiths.

As part of America's colonial society in which religious leaders were more powerful than most any other individuals, Edwards led his congregation in Northampton and much of America and Europe in the religious movement called the "Great Awakening." Like the philosopher John Locke, Edwards believed that people had to be "moved" by spiritual ideas, not just understand them—he explained it: "it is not he that has heard a long description of the sweetness of honey that can be said to have the greatest understanding of it, but he that has tasted."

Beginning in 1734 and continuing for fifteen years, this revivalism movement spread, with Edwards and his church at Northhampton as its models. In 1737, his account of the revival, *A Faithful Narrative of the Surprising Work of God*, was published in London. This launched revivals in both Scotland and England and impressed John Wesley. His abridgment of the narrative was published later and it became standard reading for Wesleyan circles.

Edwards, as one writer explains, has in contemporary times come to emerge as the man who marked the culmination of one era and "prefigured modern America." Edwards believed in the sovereignty of God in ordinary life as well as in religious observances. He believed that service to others and evangelical work among non-Christians was important. But most significant of all, Edwards was concerned with the genuine spiritual experience of salvation. One of his most popular sermons, "Heaven Is a World of Love," was part of the

---

Edwards's daily schedule began at four in the morning.

Charity and Its Fruits series of sermons he delivered in 1738. Edwards explained to his congregation: "There is in heaven this fountain of love; this eternal three in one is set open without any obstacle to hinder access to it." Edwards preached that the essence of salvation, "the covenant of grace," was a true union of the heart with Jesus, the representative of redemptive love. He followed the Calvinist belief in the perseverance of the saints, that there was no falling from the grace of God's love.

However, it is his vivid description of the consequences of the lack of a true spiritual experience that has become his most often-quoted sermon, which was first delivered in 1741. In "Sinners in the Hands of an Angry God," Edwards warned his congregation of the refusal of God's love. His lines about "hell's wide gaping mouth" and nothing being between man and eternal damnation but air and the "power and mere pleasure of God" so touched all who heard that people reportedly swooned in the aisles of the church.

As one historian notes, "with the possible exception of William Penn and Benjamin Franklin," no other colonial figure "so completely anticipated the subsequent shape of an American culture, at once material and spiritual, piously secular and pragmatically sacred, as did Edwards."

The Edwards home was in East Windsor, Connecticut. As the son of Reverend Timothy Edwards, a strict Calvinist pastor, and Esther Stoddard, the daughter of the Reverend Solomon Stoddard, a formidable and respected pastor in western Massachusetts, Edwards was greatly encouraged in his education. He was the only son, with four older sisters and six younger ones, all participating in studies. Edwards set himself apart early in his studies—he was nearly fluent in Latin by age seven. And at age 13, in 1716, Edwards entered Yale College and then continued his studies with reading theology for two years after his graduation. He is generally considered to have possessed a genius intellect.

Edwards's daily schedule began at four in the morning, with thirteen hours a day devoted to

Jonathan Edwards. Image provided by Corbis.

studying and a small time set aside for walking. He kept this routine for several years into adulthood.

Edwards also began early a strict regimen of daily prayers and Bible study and composed a list of seventy personal resolutions. The first resolution sets the stage for his life: "Resolved, that I will do whatsoever I think to be most to the glory of God."

Upon his grandfather's death, Edwards, at age twenty-three, became the minister of the thirteen-hundred-strong congregation at Northampton, Massachusetts.

Edwards's marriage to Sarah Pierrepont in 1727 was an "uncommon union," as he himself later described. He was the father of a close-knit family of eight daughters and three sons.

In 1750, Edwards was asked to leave the church in Northampton, primarily because of his adamant refusal to liberalize certain doctrinal beliefs. He spent the next seven years as a pastor in the frontier town of Stockbridge and as a missionary to Indians. Installed as president of Princeton University in 1758, he died within a few months from complications of a smallpox vaccination. An icon of strength and integrity, Jonathan Edwards remains an essential figure in the evolution of our national identity.

NAME: Jonathan Edwards

BORN: October 5, 1703, East Windsor, Connecticut

DIED: March 22, 1758, Princeton, New Jersey

ACCOMPLISHMENTS: America's greatest theologian; influential preacher and author

COLLECTOR'S CORNER

Melinda Rathjen

OLD BIBLES

As I enjoyed the post-dinner conversation at my aunt and uncle's house last Thanksgiving, a Bible displayed nearby caught my attention. The Bible, with my grandfather's name and the year 1926 engraved on its slightly worn leather cover, opens to marbled, green endsheets and a family records section. Seeing the Bible piqued my curiosity about its history and about those who have turned its pages. I wondered if others have felt the same connection to and curiosity about the past when considering their own antique Bible.

Even if no Bible has survived as your family heirloom, finding an antique Bible should not prove to be difficult. The first book to print on Gutenberg's moveable-type printing press was a Latin translation of the Bible. Since then, more copies, in more languages, have been printed of the Bible than of any other book. In addition, it has received special care throughout its history, rarely discarded or destroyed (though often worn with frequent use). Because of this production and preservation, old Bibles are readily available to match the price range of nearly anyone wishing to begin a collection.

A Bible does not need to be expensive to be interesting. As I researched my own family's Bible, I became fascinated with the history of printed Bibles, from the Gutenberg Bible to the parade of twentieth-century translations. I now cannot pick up an old Bible without wondering about its origin, its owners, and its history. Even something as commonplace as an English translation is a point of historical interest—in the fourteenth, fifteenth, and sixteenth centuries, translators were jailed, exiled, and even killed for translating the Bible into English. The Geneva Bible of 1560, for example, was a translation that was originally printed in Switzerland and smuggled into England, due to the extreme persecution in England at that time. We can examine for ourselves the victories of those and other champions of God's Word in every Bible that has since been printed.

Perhaps that is the best reason to collect old Bibles—to honor God and His people who have struggled to make His Word available to all. I am thankful for those people whose sacrifices brought us the Bible as we know it. We can read into the Bible's history, as in its pages, the love of God, who has worked through His people to speak words of grace.

In collecting editions of the Bible, one can begin to grasp the long history and importance of this Book of books. My own family's heirloom Bible, though not old or rare enough to be of great worth in dollars, is priceless to us; though not our only copy, it is the most significant. In that Bible I am able to see the legacy of printed Bibles and my own family's heritage of faith. And I am deeply grateful.

A Centuries-Old Search

Whether your family has an heirloom Bible, or you are searching for an old printing of the Bible, the following information may be useful:

Rare and Significant:

• Knowledge of the rare, historical editions will help when looking for the less costly, newer printings.

• Ten of the surviving forty-eight copies (of a print run of about 180) of the Gutenberg Bible can be found in U.S. libraries. The hypothetical value of a Gutenberg Bible in today's market is about one hundred million dollars, with even one leaf, or page, selling for more than fifty thousand dollars.

• The 1560 Geneva Bible, which has recently been offered for sale at nearly thirty thousand dollars, was the Bible of Shakespeare and the Pilgrims. It survives in fewer than fifty known copies.

• Fewer than two hundred copies are known to survive of the first edition 1611 King James, or Authorized, Version. Though not as rare or as old as the Geneva, it has been sold for as much as four hundred thousand dollars at auction. The demand is high for this edition because of its historical and literary significance and continuing popularity.

Determining Monetary Value:

• Rarity, historical significance, and market demand for a particular edition help determine value.

• Year of printing—the date is located on the general title page, the New Testament title page, or the colophon (the last page of scripture); if there is more than one date, the latest date applies.

• Bibles printed in America before 1800 or in Europe before 1700 are valued in the thousands of dollars and increase in value by as much as twenty percent per year. Those printed in America after 1800 or in Europe after 1700, however, are not likely to be worth more than a few hundred dollars.

• Size—most Bibles are "quarto" size, or about seven inches wide by about nine inches tall. Less common are the larger "folio" size Bibles ("pulpit

A manuscript illumination from the 1480 Vulgate Biblia Latina, entitled THE EXPULSION, *Newberry Library, Chicago. Image from SuperStock.*

Bibles"), approximately fifteen inches tall, and the smaller "octavo" size, approximately five inches by eight inches. Even smaller are the toy-like "thumb" Bibles, which were first popular in the 1800s.

• Collation and condition—all of the pages should be present and in good shape. (Incomplete Bibles will sometimes be split and sold as individual leaves. With leaves from historically important editions starting at around forty dollars, this is a less expensive way to own a piece of Bible history.)

• Binding condition does not negatively affect the value of an antique Bible.

Caring for Your Bible

• Store your vintage or heirloom Bible out of direct sunlight, avoiding extreme temperatures, humidity, and dust.

• Take care that unnecessary stress is not placed on the binding; do not force it to lie flat, and support the covers when open.

Not yesterday I learned to know the love of bare November days
Before the coming of the snow.
—Robert Frost

A Walk

Maud Dawson

The bright, clouded moons of October fade.
As I walk the gray days of November,
The warm fires of memory
Keep me company when the wind
Scuffs dreams down the street.

Old friends, my family, and all children
Make brittle the cares that crack
And disperse like dry leaves.
My heart holds strong and clean,
Like the fierce sun on bare limbs.

November

Elizabeth Stoddard

Much have I spoken of the faded leaf;
    Long have I listened to the wailing wind
And watched it plowing through the heavy clouds,
    For autumn charms my melancholy mind.

When autumn comes, the poets sing a dirge:
    The year must perish; all the flowers are dead;
The sheaves are gathered; and the mottled quail
    Runs in the stubble, but the lark has fled!

Still, autumn ushers in the Christmas cheer,
    The holly berries, and the ivy tree:
They weave a chaplet for the Old Year's bier;
    These waiting mourners do not sing for me!

I find sweet peace in depths of autumn woods,
    Where grow the ragged ferns and roughened moss;
The naked, silent trees have taught me this—
    The loss of beauty is not always loss!

The Garden's Last Flowers

Betty Rivera

Survivors of frost and cold,
they wave their colorful blooms
like banners of victory,
reminding us of friends
who weather the years,
flying flags of cheer.

Glade Creek Mill in Babcock State Park, West Virginia, is framed by autumn leaves. Photograph by Dick Dietrich/Dietrich Leis Stock Photography.

COUNTRY CHRONICLE

Lansing Christman

AFTER THE PAGEANTRY

The pageantry of the brightly colored leaves across the hills and valley has come to an end. Gone are the leaves of red and scarlet, the yellow and gold, the bronze and maroon. Gone are the inviting hues that lured us outdoors to witness the glory of the season.

I, for one, in this Thanksgiving season, find both peace and pleasure in my outdoor activities, especially my walks in the woodlands of deciduous trees with their barren boughs so gracefully arching the horizon. The sun streams in through the branches overhead and becomes my chandelier, hanging from the ceiling of the bright blue skies as I walk the familiar quiet paths. I can muse and meditate, and I can dream. Here in this brisk air, my thoughts are clear and refreshing, not drab and cold as some would think.

The beating wings of the partridge as it takes flight from under a hemlock catch my attention. Ahead, I may see a deer lope off away from me or a rabbit scurry among the fallen leaves. They are just cautious in a world where being shy is sometimes the safest reaction. The neighbor's hound still continues to dig energetically for whatever prize he seeks under the thin layer of leaves and snow. And the cats venture abroad only when necessary, preferring the warmth of the fireplace in the house, or, if banished, the comfortable depth of hay burrows in the barn.

The birds, who never seem to stop embracing each day's opportunities, still keep me company. The blue jays scold and the crows browse the landscape in dark curves. The chickadees and nuthatches flit quickly to the next meal; I must remember to keep the feeders near the house full the next few months. The chattering squirrels argue among themselves and race from branch to branch when irritated with their fellows. They are nature's comedians.

Each creature reminds me that there are so many tasks yet to be accomplished, that even in the steel chill of autumn's finale, life does go on. Sometimes it is necessary to remember that the muted days of early winter have their own lessons for us, if we just look and listen and accept. And with these lessons from the woodland paths, we ourselves can stand ready with strength and courage to meet the harsh winds and cold demands of the next day.

The author of four books, Lansing Christman has contributed to IDEALS *for more than thirty years. Mr. Christman has also been published in several American, international, and Braille anthologies. He lives in rural South Carolina.*

Early snow dusts an oak forest in the Siskiyou Mountains at the Cascade-Siskiyou National Monument, Oregon. Photograph by Terry Donnelly/Donnelly Austin Photography.

85

READERS' FORUM

Snapshots from our IDEALS readers

Left: This rag-topped clown is two-year-old Julia Hartman Teske, and she is serious about her snack. Her grandmother, Jean Teske of Fishkill, New York, sent this cute snapshot to us.

Right: The "Hiding Tree" is the perfect place for fall adventures with twins Justin and Jason Kempel. Their grandmother, Verla Lobdell of Lena, Illinois, shared this photograph from a recent hike.

Bottom right: This "Cook in a Pot" is six-month-old Alexander Swanson, son of Carl and Annalyn Swanson of Austin, Texas. His great-grandparents, Mary Lee and Lou Tirado of Laguna Woods, California, have seven other great-grandchildren sharing family activities.

Right: "Just my size," says two-year-old Alexis Kennedy Hopkins, while furniture shopping with her grandmother, Virginia Switzer of Louisville, Kentucky. Alexis is the daughter of Charlton and Larinda Hopkins, also from Louisville.

Below: "Don't forget me!" each duck seems to be telling Cameron James Hovland and his mother Kris, of Forest Lake, Minnesota. They, with Cameron James's sister Lauren and father Dan, are visiting great-grandparents, Jim and Magel Boyd of San Diego, California, who wrote that feeding the ducks is one of their holiday traditions.

THANK YOU for sharing your family photographs with IDEALS. We hope to hear from other readers who would like to share snapshots with the IDEALS family. Please include a self-addressed, stamped envelope if you would like the photos returned. Keep your original photographs for safekeeping and send duplicate photos along with your name, address, and telephone number to:

Readers' Forum
Ideals Publications
535 Metroplex Drive, Suite 250
Nashville, Tennessee 37211

ideals

Publisher, Patricia A. Pingry
Editor, Marjorie Lloyd
Designer, Marisa Calvin
Copy Editor, Melinda Rathjen
Permissions Editor, Patsy Jay
Contributing Writers, Marie H. Andrews, Lansing Christman, Maud Dawson, Pamela Kennedy, and Melissa Lester

ACKNOWLEDGMENTS

CARNEY, MARY LOU. "First Monday of November" from *A Month of Mondays* by Mary Lou Carney. Copyright © 1984. Published by Abingdon Press. Used by permission of the author. JAQUES, EDNA. "Thankful for What?" from *Uphill All the Way.* Copyright © 1977 by Edna Jaques. Published by Western Producer Prairie Books. Used by permission of Louise Bonnell. TABER, GLADYS. An excerpt from "November" from *Stillmeadow Calendar.* Copyright © 1967 by Gladys Taber. Published by J. B. Lippincott Company. Used by permission of Brandt & Hochman Literary Agents, Inc. Our sincere thanks to those authors, or their heirs, some of whom we were unable to locate, who submitted poems or articles to *Ideals* for publication. Every possible effort has been made to acknowledge ownership of material used.

Top: "This one, definitely this one." Logan Elizabeth Gallant, fifteen months old, is selecting her very first pumpkin. Her grandmother, Kathy Comstock of Milford, Maine, says, "She's the love of my life!"

Below: Young Joseph John Lipinski knows how to make pumpkin-picking easy—just hitch a ride! He is the son of Paul and Caroline Lipinski, of Downers Grove, Illinois, and the grandson of Len and Loretta Lipinski of Homewood, Illinois, and Richard and Felicia Bubula of Chicago.

GIVE *ideals* THIS CHRISTMAS . . . Let *ideals* express your heartfelt wishes at every season of the year!

Every issue of **Ideals** is bursting with a celebration of life's special times: Christmas, Thanksgiving, Easter, Mother's Day, Country and Friendship. Give a gift subscription to **Ideals** this Christmas and you will bring joy to the lives of special people six times a year! Each issue offers page after page of magnificent photographs, exquisite drawings and paintings, delightful stories and poetry. Each is a "keeper" that invites the reader back, again and again, to look, read and ponder. There's nothing quite as special as a gift of **Ideals**!

WE'LL SEND A GIFT ANNOUNCEMENT WITH THE FIRST ISSUE!

SAVE 44%
off the bookstore price!
To order, mail card below

Preferred Subscriber Guarantee

1. We guarantee that you may cancel your subscription(s) at any time upon request and that you will receive a prompt refund on any unserved issues.

2. We guarantee to continue your gift subscription(s) at the then current rate for as long as you wish, without interruption, unless you instruct us to stop.

3. We guarantee if you extend your own subscription we will also provide continuous service at the then current rate for as long as you wish.

4. Send no money now. As a Preferred Subscriber, a gift card will be automatically sent in your name every year (on receipt of payment) to the person named.

---

ideals CHRISTMAS GIFT LIST
PREFERRED SUBSCRIBER Guarantee

❑ **YES!** Please send a one-year *Ideals* gift subscription to my friends listed below.
❑ $19.95 enclosed for each   ❑ Bill me $19.95 for each

MY NAME:

_____
NAME

_____
ADDRESS

_____
CITY   STATE   ZIP
❑ Please also enter a subscription for myself

SEND A GIFT SUBSCRIPTION TO:

_____
NAME

_____
ADDRESS

_____
CITY   STATE   ZIP

SEND A GIFT SUBSCRIPTION TO:

_____
NAME

_____
ADDRESS

_____
CITY   STATE   ZIP

For addresses outside the U.S.A., annual rate is $25.95 for Canadian and $30.95 for Foreign, payable in U.S. funds.

05-202242703

---

ideals CHRISTMAS GIFT LIST
PREFERRED SUBSCRIBER Guarantee

❑ **YES!** Please send a one-year *Ideals* gift subscription to my friends listed below.
❑ $19.95 enclosed for each   ❑ Bill me $19.95 for each

MY NAME:

_____
NAME

_____
ADDRESS

_____
CITY   STATE   ZIP
❑ Please also enter a subscription for myself

SEND A GIFT SUBSCRIPTION TO:

_____
NAME

_____
ADDRESS

_____
CITY   STATE   ZIP

SEND A GIFT SUBSCRIPTION TO:

_____
NAME

_____
ADDRESS

_____
CITY   STATE   ZIP

For addresses outside the U.S.A., annual rate is $25.95 for Canadian and $30.95 for Foreign, payable in U.S. funds.

05-202242703

Do your Christmas shopping today and
SAVE 44%

ONLY $19⁹⁵

off the regular bookstore price of *Ideals* when you give a one-year subscription!

Everyone knows at least two or three people who would love a gift subscription to *Ideals*! It's a very special Christmas gift that keeps on reminding a close friend or relative of your thoughtfulness all through the year. And, when you order now, you enjoy a generous savings off the regular bookstore price—and do your Christmas shopping right away!

for each one-year gift subscription of six issues—a savings of $15.75 off the bookstore price.

To order today, use one or both of the postage-paid reply cards (see reverse side).

Add more gifts, if you wish, by enclosing a separate list with the additional names and addresses and mail in an envelope to:

Ideals Publications, Inc.
A Division of Guideposts
P.O. Box 796
Carmel, NY 10512-0796

SEND NO MONEY NOW—WE'LL BILL YOU LATER!

Orders received after December 1 will start with the Easter issue.